WE WERE PEDESTRIANS

WE WERE PEDESTRIANS

Gerard Woodward

Chatto & Windus
LONDON

Published by Chatto & Windus 2005

2 4 6 8 10 9 7 5 3 1

Copyright © Gerard Woodward 2005

First published in Great Britain in 2005 by
Chatto & Windus
Random House, 20 Vauxhall Bridge Road,
London SW1V 2SA

Random House Australia (Pty) Limited
20 Alfred Street, Milsons Point, Sydney,
New South Wales 2061, Australia

Random House New Zealand Limited
18 Poland Road, Glenfield,
Auckland 10, New Zealand

Random House South Africa (Pty) Limited
Endulini, 5A Jubilee Road, Parktown 2193, South Africa

Random House UK Limited Reg. No. 954009

A CIP catalogue record for this book
is available from the British Library

ISBN 0 7011 7887 6

Papers used by Random House UK Limited are natural,
recyclable products made from wood grown in sustainable forests.
The manufacturing processes conform to the environmental
regulations of the country of origin.

Typeset in Bembo by Palimpsest Book Production Limited,
Polmont, Stirlingshire

Printed and bound in Great Britain by
Mackays of Chatham plc, Chatham, Kent

For Suzanne, Corin and Phoebe

Some of these poems have appeared in – *Ambit*, *P.N.Review*, *Staple*, *Poetry Wales*, and the *TLS*. 'Giant' was commissioned by the Salisbury Last Words Poetry Festival for display in a dolls' house shop window, and appeared in the *Last Words* anthology, edited by Don Paterson and Jo Shapcott. 'Ecopoesis' appeared in *New Writing 13*, edited by Toby Lit and Ali Smith.

CONTENTS

My Father's Industry   1
The Barn   2
Pen y Bryn   3
Moorside   4
Phoebe   6
My Children Have Tails   7
House-Hunting   8
The Good Hotel   9
The Scrapyard   10
Pegasus   12
The Lavatory   14
Flush   15
Tent Perspectives   17
Shoes   18
M5   19
A Bouquet   20
Mud   22
Muddy   23
Norfolk   24
Castaway   26
Grimsby   28
North from Reykjavik   29
Scenes from Beowulf   30
Living Off The Land   34
A Proclamation   35
Slugs   36
Cow-pats Revisited   37
The House in the Aerials   38
Autumn in the Maze   40
The Swing   41
Self-Seal   43
Elephant   44
James   46
The Books   47
The Plume   48
On the Corner   50

A Saucepan with a Glass Lid   52
The Trees Have Gone Berserk   53
The Overcoat   54
Giant   56
Head   58
Dr Profundo   59
Ecopoesis   60
The Roller   71

MY FATHER'S INDUSTRY

My father's industry
Was too soft for words,
Too weak to sink shafts
Or raise chimneys. Instead
There were hollows,
Small carved caves,
Heaps of shale that
Could pass for dead leaves,
Unnoticed in a beauty spot of leaning
Birches and dripping cliffs.
The spoil was hardly rock at all,
More like the petrified fill
Of pillows, floss, baby clothes.
Though there was a kiln,
Whose cracks fired spears of red heat
That lit up the wood at night,
And which could burn for years.

THE BARN

His football boomed against the big
Iron barn where the sheep wintered.
He told us his father was dead.

We were shocked when he gave us the figures;
Five hundred sheep, a hundred and fifty
Cows – where were they all?

I filled the evenings with my first jigsaw
In thirty years, a thousand creepy
Pieces of a Scottish Castle with too much sky,

And when I finally found some old newspaper
To light the fire, its front page announced
The safe return of the first men on the moon.

There were more wardrobes in our wing
Than seemed necessary, sometimes two
To a room, great walnut monsters

From between the wars, offering their
Chambered interiors like nautili
In cross-section. The servants' bells

Slept in their disconnected coils.
And the little boy insisted with a grin
That his father was dead, and so

We didn't ask about the man
Who three times a day filled the feeding
Troughs with brass-coloured meal

And who every night I saw going over his flock
One last time before turning out the light
In that enormous room.

PEN Y BRYN

Later, she believed someone
Had stolen her bathroom
And would show anyone passing
The empty space it had once

Filled, a scrubby patch at the side
Of her cottage, the site
Of a wood shed long since felled,
But we'd listen anyway

In the grip of her arthritic hand,
How they'd come in the night
And taken the whole lot –
Bath, sink, pumice stones,

Loofahs, her medicines,
Support rails and towel rails,
Mirrors, walls, everything.
After a while I found myself

Going out of my way to avoid her,
Taking instead the route
Through the allotments
With all their slaughtered cauliflowers,

Or sometimes the other way,
Behind her cottage onto the hillside,
Past the old workings, where I'd
Sometimes pause at a cleft in the rock

Where once they'd hauled out buckets
Of slag and ore, and hear
An echoey sound within, like
Someone running a bath and singing.

MOORSIDE

We were in love for the whole of July.
She took me to her house by the moors
And I lived as her guest until she died.

By then the heather was gross with flowers
And crowded with its invisible fruit,
The soon-to-be-shot grouse, who moved
Like children under a duvet.

I covered her with a purple sheet.
The month of our lives was still
Sharp in my heart; the parachute
Display where we met, those
Men falling out of the sky, the slow

Blubber of their chutes falling behind them.
One, I remember, was lifted back
Into the air by a sudden gust after landing
And was whipped back onto the ground
Where he broke like a toy.

Her wake was set against the fattening
Of the moors, the antennae-twitch
Of tall sprigs registering the below-
Flowers blundering of birds.

On the third day of her stillness
We were overrun by crowds of black flies
Who dragged long, crippled legs beneath them.
I wished I'd known her father,
An inventor of modern adhesives.
He'd once stuck himself to the outside
Of a biplane to prove a point.

I thought I might sink in a mire of ripe grouse.
One night I dreamt I'd pulled
The sheet back from her body
To find it was made entirely of birds –
A roosting, elderly pheasant for her head
With two attentive, listening wheatears,
Her neck was a brace of bitterns
And two trembling partridges were her breasts
Beneath which the pulse of a cornered robin knocked,
That they all took flight in an instant,
Filling the room with their stupid soaring,
Crashing into my face as though I wasn't there.

I left in the middle of August.
She'd been taken by relatives
To a cemetery in the province of her father's people.
I closed the house and passed through
Its rusted gate to the lane,
To the rise and fall of the grouse,
The faltering heartbeat of the guns.

PHOEBE

Not knowing how she is named
For a shepherdess, in the clough
She converses easily with sheep,
Lambs especially, being on their level.
She finds a voice for them,
Which she produces fluently.
On the path out of the mountains
That leads us through a scattered
Flock of eighty or more, she bleats
At a lamb, who bleats back.
We ask her what it was saying
And she translates its talk as though
Surprised we couldn't understand
Its simple cry – 'I am a baby! I am a baby!'

MY CHILDREN HAVE TAILS

Mankind is one. All men belong to the same species.
(UNESCO declaration, 1949)

They come racing downstairs,
Burst into the room, yelling
'We've got tails, we've got tails . . .'
Long ribbons hitched into the backs
Of their trousers trailing
Nervelessly after them,
One purple, one gold.

Are they cats or comets,
Or an imagined, fabled species
Such as one of Linnaeus's time
Claimed to have seen in Africa,
Or Pliny in Ceylon,
Or Marco Polo in Sumatra
Whose men had holes
In their chairs to accommodate
A palm's length of appendix?

It always turns to bitterness.
She seems in real agony when he rips
Her tail right out of her spine,
Discards it. And later, when my misplaced
Foot docks his, a sudden sense
Of his being cut down, lopped,
Fallen before his time.

When the little storm of their playing
Has retreated back up the stairs
I find the two tails on the floor,
The tracks of shooting stars frozen,
Solid pulses of energy that I pick up
And pocket. I need to remember them.
Where they came from.

HOUSE-HUNTING

This is about how houses
Stand alone in that moment
Between policies, keys, curtains,

When furniture has shed
Its last bail of flesh
And enjoys its uselessness,

And meaning is unhooked
From its tacks and hangers
To revel in misalignment.

It is about how living,
Dwelling, inhabiting become
Forgotten skills marked

By traces left in pathless
Tracts, how each room
Opens like a diorama

Of geological time,
Where light-switches
Seem out of place – little

Plaques commemorating touch.
Rawlplugs pupate
In their drilled nooks,

Frail roots of blu-tac
Adhere with blind faith
As if they'd been grown there.

It is about how absence
Is built up, layer
Upon layer, how

It sediments in
Stairwells, alcoves, to form
Exquisite, unworkable rock.

THE GOOD HOTEL

Mr Bridge showed us round the property.
His mouth was a trap-door
Made of skin. I kept thinking
I might fall into it.

'The town needs a good hotel,'
He said, 'There are seventeen bedrooms here,
Wonderful views from each one.'
The windows were like trap-doors

Into which mountains and an estuary
Had fallen. How much, we thought,
Would seventeen bedrooms cost? Seventeen
Mirrors. Seventeen televisions. 'Children come

From everywhere,' he said, 'for the crab fishing.'
From a window we could see them, lined
Up along the quay with plumb lines
Picking at the water,

Lifting the crabs who waved hello
As they ascended. 'The children
Teach the grown ups,' Mr Bridge said,
And I thought how the estuary

Was a trapdoor down which the moon
And sea had fallen, a ping-pong
Ball in a blue silk handkerchief.
Mr Bridge sneezed into his wrist.

Seventeen cakes of soap, we thought.
Seventeen duvets. Then the overheads.
The damp. 'Our town deserves a good
Hotel,' Mr Bridge said, yawning.

THE SCRAPYARD

Nearly every day we pass the scrapyard
With its wedding cakes of cars
Overspilling a narrow strip
Between workshops and ordinary houses,
Where suddenly a stretch of even pavement
Breaks down, cracked and pitted
By the impacts of delivered salvage,
Passed over by the waggle-dance
Of a small forklift, dwelt in
By an Alsatian that lolls tongue-out
As though pissed, or who else
Trots freely a range of backstreets,
So that it is somewhere we tread carefully
In passing, especially when the silent parties
Of grimy men loiter on their rugs
Of trodden-in sump-oil, sometimes
With their manly children, though
They wait with the edgy courtesy
Of chauffeurs outside a church.

The cars have been stripped
Of any capacity for motion.
Wheels off, their little brake drums
Seem shockingly exposed, like
Limb buds, or the stumps
Of limb-pulled insects, while
Their engines stand uselessly
Beside them, little Mayan temples
Of steel, open-headed, revealing
Hidden depths. As humiliating
As a strip and search, more so.
More like something seen
On Traitor's Gate, or Kurtz's
Station – tribal, brutal, dark . . .

Think of what brought them here though,
Some have taken the full brunt of a head-on,
Completely flayed of their crumple zones,
Still with a drizzle of blood on the dash,
Or else deployed airbags hanging impotently,
Having delivered their one instant dream,
While the lucky ones have just slipped away
Having tottered to the supermarket
With a family of four on their backs
For the last time. And you think
How even the poorest wreck began life
In a dazzling showroom, its purchase
Agonised over, wrangled over, of all
The cajoling and smooth-talking, the haggling
Over percentages, extended warranties,
The little extras thrown in that it took
To eventually get them through the door.
Like I said, it is a place we only ever see
In passing. You can't look for long.

PEGASUS

When we met, the daddy-long-legs
Must have been in season
Because they'd gather in the clumps
Of marram grass at the back
Of her cottage and tie themselves
Up in knots with each other.
In the evenings, strolling through
Her little gate onto the hillside,
We'd come across these
Gatherings, the flies in a kind
Of silent hysteria, like tiny
Wrestlers holding each other
Down on the mat, waiting
For the count.
We'd get down on our knees
To observe their intimacies,
Fascinated, suddenly,
By this micro-fucking,
Wondering how it worked,
If we could see the vital elements
Combining. What we felt,
However, was embarrassment.
It was like sauntering into
A country church to find
A service actually going on,
Bowed heads and genuflections,
That made you want to turn around
And pretend you'd never been there.

I still remember her cottage.
Sometimes the daddy-long-legs got in
And hung precariously on the
Flaking plaster on her bathroom
Ceiling which meant you could
Study them almost clinically,
Be face to face with them,

Stare into their lollipop eyes,
Admire their crème brulée
Wings, their sea-horse snouts.

The nights were so dark
You'd think the sun
Was never coming back.
I'd sometimes lie in the bed
Kept awake by this noise
That was probably the central
Heating fluttering into life,
But which I sometimes took
For the impatient stretching
And beating of an enormous
Pair of wings, white-quilled
And magnificent, that might
Have belonged to a stabled
Horse, had she had horses,
Or stables.

THE LAVATORY

Hardly counting as a room,
Enough space to fit
A person seated. Above them
A ledge of water bracketed
To the lilac wall. Water
That also sat and waited,
That was secretly full of leverage.

Not really a room,
A place where we achieved
Sea-level, where we sat
Weighed, weighing less,
In the pan of the scales
That always balanced.

More a place between rooms
Where we paused between selves.
A place of mixed waters,
Hardly known, yet the route
To it always on the tips
Of our tongues, should a stranger
Ask for it. Any stranger who went there
Might return as a friend.

FLUSH

The knack of the water
Was in the way you pulled
The chain, like a bell ringer
At matins, evensong, a wedding,

And then to watch the arrival
In the pan of the combing
Flush, crowded like sand
At the bell-waist of an egg-timer,

Then the rising froth,
The opened magnum,
A boiling weir like a tidal
Bore that meant water

Had fallen through its trapdoors
To the third of its stations
Through the house, to throng
In that narrow villa of porcelain

Where you were just moments ago.
It takes a minute for things
To settle. The cistern
Refills like an old lady

Pouring tea, and then, when
The foam has evened out,
There is nothing but a well
Of lucid, inviting water

Where before there had been a glut
Of tidal mud. How this spring
Takes you and takes you whole,
Busily tidies you. It is like the trick

Of the hazelnut under
The three cups. You suspect
Sleight of hand, a switch
To have taken place. But it is

Intermediate water. Water that
Sits and waits. You could draw
A glassful, hold it to the light
And watch the lions playing.

TENT PERSPECTIVES

A day later and we still found
The stairs a novelty.

Glass in the windows, upper floors,
Electrics – these all seemed risky things

After ten days on Skye in a four-man tent.
We still had our tent-selves,

Heating tins for our supper,
Not understanding the television

And feeling always that things
Needed weighing down

In case a breeze should take them.
But no breeze comes in a house.

The walls don't have that twitchiness.
The floors always find their level.

It wasn't like that on Trotternish,
Pitched on a slope so we rolled

Like skittles in our sleep,
Woke in a puddle and had the birds

Scratching in our porch.
Not until the tent

Was put to sleep in the loft
After a week of airing

And the last Skye grass
Was sucked from the carpet

Did our house-selves come back to us,
Partly welcome. Almost familiar.

SHOES

As he outgrows each pair of shoes,
From mouse-like pumps
To embryonic trainers, sparkling
Jelly shoes, teddy bear slippers,

I take them and I burn them,
Funneling the ashes and oily
Residues of each into a stoppered
Glass jar and range them on a shelf,

The level of cinders increasing
With each, so that I have a broken
Path in my mind, of every
Step he's taken up till now.

M5

He'd build me a house.
He'd build it himself, he said.

I met him on the cement bus
That went past the works

On its way to my school,
Though he was working on the motorway

At the time. He said it was like
Building the world, and told

Me about the orchards they'd lifted,
The dinosaurs they'd found,

The churches they'd had to move
Stone by stone, each numbered.

North to south the motorway ran
Through our parishes, and his

Overalls were stacked with the interior
Clays he and his gangs had scooped.

He took me back to his caravan,
Set me up in a boudoir

Of grease guns, car jacks,
Other tools. He promised

To build me a house,
He'd build it himself, he said.

A BOUQUET

Interflora left us a note
Saying the flowers had been left
At No. 19.

I knocked. No one answered.
The doorway smelt of piss.
Felt-tipped graffiti filled the porch.

They hadn't been there long –
A few months. We kept
Out of their way, avoiding

Their needful smiles in the morning,
Not wanting to get hooked
Into their support networks

Lending first sugar,
Then money – our entire lives ...
It had happened before.

So we watched instead
From the middle distance
Of our windows

And answered only one approach
When the mother asked for a pound
To buy bread at midnight,

Though sometimes the toddler
Would knock and ask us
Where she lived.

Otherwise it was dealers,
Creditors, welfare officers, the police,
A man with an iron bar

Who woke us with their visits
Two doors down . . .
And then they were gone.

The door, kicked in,
Was boarded up,
Though we still saw the woman.

She must have borrowed
A room somewhere nearby,
Or a house, while theirs

Stayed nailed shut.
And so I wonder about the flowers,
If they ever found something

To put them in.
Whether they watered them.
Did they get in the way

Of the television or the door?
What did they make of them?
How long did they live?

MUD

Tempted from the path
By a reach of mud
That filled a space
Between the tough grasses
Of the plateau; thinking,
Almost, that a man
Was lying belly-down
In the turf, so back-smooth,
Porous and tense, like
The curled shoulders
Of a sprinter in his blocks,
Ten seconds of madness
Waiting in each cell
Of muscle, ten seconds
Unfurling a lifetime of preparation,
He stepped onto it.
The mud twitched in response,
Sweat beaded the outline
Of his boot. Beneath his boot
He felt the mud start.

MUDDY

My son's full nappy
Has the reassuring weight
Of a loaded slingshot, or a sandbag
Set against an insistent flood.

In its nook is laid
A muddy path, a view
Of February fields
Like the ones we walked through

Today on our muddy walk, when we
Tried to skirt ditch-mud, or slip
In single file around the loose hems
Of ploughlands. I can see

Our footprints, in the same way
He saw footprints in a cow-pat,
Tiny ones, tracing our own path
Through a circular landscape . . .

The weight of his nappies
Now forms the brunt
Of our rubbish. I totter
Like Atlas with them to the bin.

NORFOLK

1

All along this coast
They use beach pebbles
To face the buildings,
So that whole villages
Seem dressed in a single
Suit of blistered armour

Or like something a child
Might build in an afternoon
On the shingle,
His knees raw,
His fingernails dry.

2

In the arcades, small change
Is nudged ever closer
To an edge, until it
Overhangs impossibly.

My son becomes obsessed
With adding to their hoard,
One coin at a time, each,
When settled, pushed by
Gentle machinery into
The common crowd of moneys
Who always find room for it.

Then, to my amazement,
He wins a pound's worth of 2p's.

3

In the week of our residence
His tooth finally came out,
The first of twenty,
Whose fall came after weeks
Of an enticing looseness,
An increasing foldability,
Until it seemed held in place
By nothing more than shyness.

A sweetly bloodied mouth,
Then a visit from the tooth fairy
Stupid with whisky
Whose pound was converted
First thing the next morning
Into fifty two-pence pieces
And fed to the machines,
Lost in a matter of minutes.

4

'I didn't win, Dad,' he said, shocked
As we walked on the beach afterwards.
The pebbles jostled and clucked
Beneath our feet.
'I didn't win.'

CASTAWAY

A house so cold I slept
In a pyramid of quilts

And coats. The chill was delivered
By the convection of a small river

That flowed beside the garden
Murmuring like a dinner party,

Drowsy after its fall, two miles back,
Where it entered the valley

Through a trapdoor, then a hundred
And fifty feet of slate.

The next cottage was sandbagged.
In the short evenings I played

Soccer with my kids
And miskicked the ball

Into the stream, so that it bobbed
Happily out of our lives,

Like Wilson, in *Castaway*.
My son cried, as he'd almost

Cried at the film when Tom
Hanks's confidant, a football

With a human face, a shock
Of twigs for hair and a look

Of rigid indifference, even
To its own, drifting fate,

Dribbled off the raft.
We followed ours as far

As we could, over a fence,
Through a copse, but were soon

At the limits of the property.
The river, in its hurry to be

Elsewhere, had taken our ball
All the way to the sea, we supposed,

And might soon be buoyed
On a frothy crest of the Pacific,

Or washed up on a sweetly
Reeking shore in humid regions . . .

We returned to the cottage
As though from the docks

That had taken the children
To war. Spent the rest

Of the night trying
To get the damn fire going.

GRIMSBY

Since you ask, I've never paid for sex.
Instead, when I'm asleep and cold,
She lifts the easy money from my slacks.

I have become accustomed to her tricks
On the waterfront where she patrols.
Since you ask, I've never paid for sex.

The fish are lifted from the smacks,
Herrings taken from the fold.
She lifts the easy money from my slacks.

We sip V8 by the moonlit docks
And watch our future lives unfold.
Since you ask, I've never paid for sex.

She says it's time I made some tracks,
My fish have all been sold.
She lifts the easy money from my slacks.

I slip into my icy anorak
And leave to hunt the Arctic shoals.
Since you ask, I've never paid for sex,
She lifts the easy money from my slacks.

NORTH FROM REYKJAVIK

We walked all day in our wellingtons
To see the northern whaling stations.

Our feet were bleeding in their rubber
When we saw the slipways full of blubber,

Men slicing into pouches,
Dissecting hearts as big as couches,

Entrails drying on the beaches,
Pink blood foaming in the reaches.

In the town we sensed hostility,
Couldn't even get a cup of tea.

Hungry, we walked back across the lava,
My friend seemed able to walk for ever

Though I felt a void beneath my jumper.
'Portrait of a person in a fucking awful temper,'

He said, framing me as we walked
In a square of fingers. We never talked

After that, until we got to Reykjavik
At dawn. And then I was sick.

SCENES FROM BEOWULF

1. The Funeral

Why bring me to this ship,
Hold me to the sea's edge
On the crowd's shoulder,
Naked as a sword? It was
My time. I'd fed my last.
Fat, fit to sleep for ever,
My long rule over, I was
A child again. The boat
Arched against the hazardous
Eddies. I was placed
In its heart, in a nest
Of weaponry, for the tide
To lift to the deep
Swell and sealing-off
From life. I slept in the lull
Of its pitiful crises,
Fell into the crashed
Machine of its nursery,
To be hauled out by whom?

2. The Time Capsule

Our time had come.
I took what was left –
Plated vessels, cups,
Helmets inlaid
With shell, a cuirass,
Broken shields, shirts,
A harp, and filled
A hollow in the ground
And lived above its
Silent presence. Final
Earl, my earldom
Everything, for a while.
I spent my time
Picturing its refinding,
Our flowering long fallen,
What company might
Delve and shift
Mud from a glinting
Edge and pick out
Cup after cup, our
Masks, might even
Drink again, fill
A hall with song,
Bring the movement
Of swift horses
To our motionless gold?

3. The Arming

Indifferent to life,
I withdrew into a shell
Of metal, my shirt
A miracle of crocheted iron,
My heart sounded
In its curdled halls,
My brain excelled
In its silver academy.
I was multi-smithied
Into a walking treasure,
Wonderfully made,
A whole troop, I stood
Like the city of gold,
Or the wind-ranged,
Ocean-hammered cliffs
At the world's end.

Until that grappling
With blood on the sea floor
When my sword became
A single tusk of ice,
And my whole self plated
With the vagrancy
Of the long-frozen,
Which thawed.

And in the vernal light
After battle my naked
Core was revealed,
The stump of my weapon
Still in my hand.

4. The Hoard

Still warm from battle, what
Was hidden now is naked, the hoard
They fought over here bright
On the ground, the serpent
Having withdrawn into its coils
Of blood, into silence. The legacy
Of a vanished race, gold cups raised
But empty, ornaments askew,
Rusted helmets heaped,
Arm rings twisted, threatening.
All was lit by a standard
Woven wonderfully in gold
Making bright this plunder.
Suddenly I thought of the man
Who set it there, staggering
Through the hewn earth, tilting
Under the weight of gold,
Fat with it, until he fell.

LIVING OFF THE LAND

By the time the new general arrived
Our officers were wearing camel skins,
The hussars were half starved.

Horses were left unshod.
They hadn't seen grass for months.
The blowflies sipped our blood.

'You haven't been paid for two years,'
He said in his first address,
'We can make up the arrears.

Before us lie the riches
Of the desert, its secret palaces
Where honey flows in the ditches.

I can promise ten pounds of hay
For the horses. A gallon of water
And a bushel of oats a day . . .'

'There is nothing but sand
Between here and the Tigris,'
A subaltern said, raising a hand.

'Even in sand there is wealth,'
The general replied, his charger stirring,
'And we can find our food in filth.

The war shall feed our war,
Wheat-fields grow where blood falls . . .'
It was what we wanted to hear.

That night the moon fell
Into a trance above the ruins
Of that long-abandoned citadel.

A PROCLAMATION

Soldiers! In fifteen days
You have won six victories,
Taken twenty-one oil wells,
Fifty-five factories,
Several mosques.
You have knocked the devil
Out of his socks.
The sands around are level.

Deprived of everything
You have made up for everything.
You have won battles without radar,
Scaled keeps without ladders.
You have forded the deepest rivers.
You have built bridges.

Now we are at the gates
Of the city, swords drawn.
Our mules munch their dates
And our camels yawn.
One last piece of advice –
You remember how
We tip-toed through paradise?
Tread quietly now.

SLUGS

By thinking of the slugs
As black or ginger cats
Asleep on concrete couches,
He'd domesticated them.

No more of those tiny bulls,
Menacing slicks of muscle,
Of the type picadors tease,
Whose horns always seemed

Pointed in his direction,
Nor thoughts of the vulnerable
Midriff of Prometheus
On the patio at twilight.

But then his wife ruined it,
Sighting dolphins
Breaking the surf of the path
With their playful faces.

COW-PATS REVISITED

The black cows steeped
In dandelions.

The turmeric-coloured flies
Steeped in cow-pats.

The cows have produced
Their own inverse Lilliputs.

Visiting them I find bronze
Cows hock-deep in black

Dahlias. These cows
Produce golden filth

That falls and falls
Into the black shrub

Like the meltdowns of trophies
To produce a second

Inversion, peopled as they are
By tiny black flies,

Whose near presence
Reveals them as slow,

Prurient, confused creatures
Steeped in dandelions.

THE HOUSE IN THE AERIALS

When the first aerial arrived
We treated it as a joke –
A mast without its ship
Filling a window,

But with the further aerials
That came over the following
Months and years,
The joke thinned,

And when I last visited
Her cottage – the highest
In the county, perched on a ridge
Of bleached granite, it seemed

In a forest of transmitters
And receivers of varying
Sizes – some little more than
Tent poles stripped of their canvas,

Others vast ladders to heaven,
Or so they appeared in low cloud.
She didn't seem to know
How they'd arrived or why,

And claimed they'd grown,
Like the beanstalk, overnight,
But then I found the unopened letters
In her drawer, franked *Ministry*

Of Defence, Orange, Home Office,
BBC, which must have given
Their warnings or sought permissions,
But which contained, to my amazement,

Cheques, standing orders, rental agreements –
She was rich, her money problems solved.
She wept when I explained,
And looked up at the highest mast

Whose top was lost in mist,
And we both felt we could see
The soles of bare feet
Nervously making their descent.

AUTUMN IN THE MAZE

The leaves are falling in the maze
And so we can't be truly lost
Now we can see through all its walls.

People think you're telling lies
When you say this fall will be your last,
The leaves are falling in the maze.

It is the emptiness that most appals,
Those spiral paths have turned to dust
Now we can see through all its walls.

This season is the cruellest phase,
Your gardeners weep, they feel abused,
The leaves are falling in the maze.

As kids we loved its secret halls,
We all had sundials in our hearts,
Now we can see through all its walls.

To the disappointed children's cries
You say it'll grow again, it must.
The leaves are falling in the maze,
Now we can see through all its walls.

THE SWING

I'm remembering the swing,
Two A's of rusted iron
Joined by horizontals.
No seat, not even the chains
That held a seat
But a fused coupling
On the top cross-bar
That must have once rooted
The moving parts, have given
The squeak, squeak of hanging
Weight grinding back and forth,
And where a cousin
I no longer know once hung
By his calves like a trapeze
Artist, his fluffy 60s hair spilling
Down, the money, the penknife,
The lighter falling into the grass.

In my time it was a climbing
Frame only, a ship from whose
Tipsy crow's nest I could peep
Into a hundred gardens,
Or sometimes a delicate,
Hollow-limbed landing craft
From which I'd nervously step
Onto the overgrown lawns
Of the moon. Then an ingenious
Lighthouse untroubled by
The violent waves passing through,
Or a weather station
For ever beneath the hammock-bulging,
Easily-understood skies whose
Rain brought out the flintiness
Of the swing, the richness
Of its withered metal, so that
I carried, always, a smell of money
Into the house.

What happened to it?
It must have passed away
With all the other things I outgrew,
Like the betrayed shirts and
Windcheaters that lay around in empty-
Sleeved shock at their sudden
Abandonment, for a while, before
Making an embarrassed, unnoticed exit.
My father must have taken the swing
In hand at some point.
An awkward thing to carry,
He must have stood inside it,
Taken hold of the cross-bar of each A
And lifted the whole thing,
As one piece, walking with it.
He must have worn it like an overcoat,
An emperor in his new clothes.
I wish I'd seen it.

SELF-SEAL

Is it something about the tongue,
These envelopes and stamps
We no longer have to lick
But which, simply by folding,
Somehow meld into themselves,
A smug, self-regarding origami?

The art of poking the tongue
To seal a letter, to fix a stamp,
May soon belong with leech-
Medicine and the eating
Of placentas, to an age
Of unhygienic romance.

To leave our hereditary material
In the seams of our missives,
To smash the thousand little silver
Padlocks of someone's spittle
To open a letter – how seed-
Scatteringly profligate, what a waste of matter!

I'll miss it, that strip
Of dried protein, most frugal
Of meals, that made communication
Into an act of intimate touching,
Even if it was just a counterfoil
We were posting, along with a cheque.

And I think of suckling pups,
Their eyelids yet to break,
Whose tongues seem their every sense,
Or myself and my mother at the school
Gates when she applied that spat-upon tissue
To something on my face that must have troubled her.

ELEPHANT

When I'm bored I visit my girlfriend
At the zoo and we feed
Her she-elephant together.

And as every apple we lob
With netball-accuracy falls into that
Ace of hearts mouth, another problem

Almost disappears (what her mother
Thinks of us, what the bank
Thinks of us, how we will ever

Have children . . .) Whole fruit
We throw – apples with stalks
And leaves, and the elephant's mouth

Is all lips and soft palate,
No tongue or visible teeth
(Though there must be some)

Just this orchid-rich pit
Of flesh. Sometimes an apple
Will bounce right out again, and crack

Open on the piss-damp cement,
Or they will bob and wobble
On her floppy lip for a heart-

Stopping second before falling in,
Then her mountainous head will nod,
Her childishly freckled trunk

Will lift and wave,
And I'll picture the summer
We first spent together

(I mean my girlfriend and I)
The sweltering afternoons we lay
On her bed, naked, side by side,

Drinking cider and exchanging
Histories, knowing we could stay there
For ever, if it wasn't for our hunger.

JAMES

I was the bait in one of his traps.
He blew a butterfly tongue of smoke
From his vinegary lips,
While I polished off his chips.

And afterwards, the green tang
Of lime sorbet,
Landing on my tongue.
He bought me a ring.

His grip grew tighter.
He whispered into his watch,
Told me his pen was mightier
Than a sword, and lighter,

And he sang me across The Lido
In his rollicking Gondola,
Took me with a glass dildo,
Taught me judo.

Do you remember Venice in the 60s, James,
Somewhere between the sea and sky?
Our home movies went up in flames,
Ashes now, or so it seems.

THE BOOKS

For the dead – paper.
The bookishness of our funerals
Became a talking point,
A reason for visiting.

Cutting and pasting crowns
Of virgin newsprint, frocks
Of A4, cartridge paper.
Our processions were acts

Of mass origami, in our creased
Clothes made sharp with thumbnails,
And the deceased dressed
In envelopes, writing paper,

Ivory laid paper, deckle-
Edged, each clean sheet
Having survived the awesome
Pounds per square inch

Of the paper mills. Afterwards,
The intimate rustling of the wake
Finished, we'd undress, carefully,
Without tearing, a mutual

Unfolding, smoothing out.
Our funeral clothes were brought
Together, stitched and bound
Into books, apparently wordless.

THE PLUME

The Dean complained to the manager
Of the power station on the opposite
Side of the river – 'Your smoke, of late,'
He said, 'doesn't seem to have the lift
It once had. Whereas before I'd watch
The sometimes almost vertical ascension
Of your sulphurous filth, to take its place
Among the clouds or, on days of high
Pressure, to be the only cloud in the sky
And spread, on finding its own level,
A beige mantle across our city
From suburb to suburb, nowadays
It comes from your chimney like
A shambling, exhausted, put-upon worm
Barely able to lift itself from the abyss
Or clear the fascinating brickwork
Of its own housing, and drags itself
Like a thing in chains, bloated, ponderous,
Pitiful, across the currents and, if the wind
Is right (or wrong, which it usually is),
Will crawl up to the south door
Of our cathedral, as though it wants
Admittance, and sometimes I wonder
If I should let it in, to flop exhausted
On a pew, give it communion, absolution,
Bless it. But usually I shut the door
And the windows too. So instead it climbs
The stonework and blackens the statuary.
Our tableau of St Paul at the Apostolic Council
Has taken the brunt. I've seen his face up close,
It's like an apple eaten to the core.
All our cherubs are weeping soot.
If things go on like this our very fabric
Will shrivel down to nothing. I ask you
To think about what you are doing to us.'

The manager of the power station replied –
'It is true our plume doesn't always
Climb the way it used to, but this is the result
Of new regulations governing sulphur emissions.
We have to wash our flue with chalky water.
This takes out ninety-nine per cent of the sulphur,
But cools the smoke as it climbs the chimney.
This coolness robs our plume of its buoyancy
In air. It cannot rise. It shambles, as you say,
Barely higher than the chimney that emitted it.
What can we do? I'm sorry about your statues
But our smoke won't nibble at their crystals
Any more. It's non-corrosive now, you see.
You're not the only one to complain.
When the wind blows the other way
A hospital slams its windows shut or else
Suffers a universal chestiness. It's the price
We have to pay for Scandinavian trees.
And what about the poor souls who gave their
Lives to the building of this place? Should they
Have died for nothing? The only alternative
Would be to switch the whole damn thing off,
And then where would our city be?

ON THE CORNER

Its reverential hush
Broken only by the entrance bell
Worked by a pressure-pad
Beneath the doormat
(A distant relative
Of the land-mine)
You meet first the bottled
Miracles mirrored to infinity,
A lake of wine that could never drain,
Then the tang of recently extinguished
Candles, unvacuumed carpets
And the Mediterranean whitewash
Which Mr Peters used to mock up
The vaults of a Spanish vintner's
Or a cellar in Oporto – Romanesque
Archways sprigged with wrought iron,
Dummy barrels of Domeque,
Plastic vines, blackboards, Bulls' Blood . . .
You solve a maze of sherry
Pyramids, bulwarks of Party Sevens
Recalling the man who scientifically
Measured the damage a bull
In a china shop actually caused
And found them to be rigid and shy
With formality when surrounded
By Spode, cracking not a single cup,
And make it to the counter
In the silent triumph a champion
Coin-balancer feels, only to find
An absence where Mr Peters was
And a map.

'He had to have a break,' she says,
Swaddling your wine and glancing
At the wall where a map
Of Offa's Dyke is pinned. A flag

Marks the last known position
Of Mr Peters. 'He needed a rest
From the lorries, they're doing
His heart in. Every time one
Comes to the corner he steps
On a brake pedal under the counter.'
(The whole shop chimes when
The lorries pass.) 'One day
It's going to happen. It just takes
One driver to sneeze at the vital
Moment, or to have a stroke
When they're turning right
And they're in through the window . . .'

Leaving, you step into a puddle
Of sound, the undiscriminating
Bell that gives equal voice
To entrances and exits. And you wonder
If it will ever happen – Mr Peters,
Knapsack on his back, leaning into
A bracing headwind on Hergest
Ridge, while in London a juggernaut
Dozes his frontage and hammers
Into his booze, each bottle of red
Wine popping like a blood blister
Until the very counter where Mr
Peters would have been standing
Is flattened beneath the wheels.
Probably not.

A SAUCEPAN WITH A GLASS LID

This is water with intent,
Water full of ladders,
Jailbreak water I've
Found a window on,
Hurling grappling irons
To monkey up, thinking
I can't see it. It is
An unlawful assembly
Standing in quaking heights
Like display motorcyclists.
And when I lift the lid
Everything is stowed,
A crowd disappears, blunt
Instruments are sleeved,
And water looks at me
With wide-eyed innocence,
Loitering, not caring,
Shuffling, whistling.
It's laughable. Ha ha.
Water and I, we laugh
Together. Ha ha. Ha ha.

THE TREES HAVE GONE BERSERK

The nerves of the trees
Are under strain. The apple

Tree's apples are now cherry-sized.
The pear tree is out of proportion,

So tall her fruit can kill
If it falls from the upper boughs.

I blame unusual weather.
Why else would the oak,

Admittedly old, leaf
At Christmas, his terrified

Acorns shiver? As if
One sun was not enough,

The efficiency of the seasons
Is in the balance. The holly

Has lost his faith
And no longer hurts.

You cannot trust
The trees any more.

The cherry will smile
And offer her hand

Hoping to smear you with blackfly.
The Warwickshire Drooper, eager

To please, came up with so many
Plums it broke her neck.

The trees are in a sour mood.
The poplar does nothing but slam doors,

Thousands of tiny ones
That fall off their hinges.

THE OVERCOAT

I am wearing such a huge overcoat.
It would keep you warm even in Antarctica.

I have been wearing it for such a long time
I am not sure what it looks like,

Or what shop it came from. I can't remember
Buying it. I've always worn it.

But I know its feel – smooth like silk,
The lining, with a smell of roast dinners.

Its weight, so heavy it seems to propel
Itself when I'm out walking, like a soft car

Or caravan. It's red inside, I think. I love
My overcoat. I would wear it even in deserts.

It has a sort of life of its own. For instance,
A sleeve might rise to a salute

Half way through a silent and lonely breakfast,
Or the two arms might fold when I want

To shake hands, or the hood
Cover my head even after the rain's gone.

Things appear in its pockets I haven't bought.
I even wear it to my frequent bed.

To tell you the truth, I'm not sure
If I can stop wearing my overcoat.

The buttons are so fast and big, to undo
Them might be my own undoing.

I would rather snuggle down beneath
The neck like something on a Tudor stair

And sleep deep in its woven insides.
But I must undress sometime.

I am putting on weight, and my overcoat
Isn't getting any bigger. But the trouble is,

I'm not sure if I am wearing it, or it
Is wearing me, and I think I might

Have to wait until it undoes itself,
Or should I try first? It's very hard,

But one of us must start.
And is it warm or cold outside?

GIANT

Six months in the north
And I have burgled the dolls' house,
My hands through the windows
Like a scientist handling
Uranium gloved, through a wall,
     But my fingers still burn

When I think of them filling
Those little rooms. Midnight
And they were still awake.
I can't sleep for what I've done.
My prints big as rugs
     On those untrodden floors.

I could go south again,
Back to the ordinary houses.
It was when I unhasped the frontage
And found it opened like a book
That I nearly fainted,
     Rooms dissected, an exploded view

Of unwanted intimacy,
Those blindly alert faces.
The sadness of my heist
Hit me when I emptied
My pockets, for they contained
     Absurdities – a pill-sized

Light bulb, chairs upholstered
In moleskin that wouldn't seat
A rat, chandeliers like ear rings,
A fingernail diadem. I can't
Return them. The whole house
     Slammed shut. I ran.

I stayed two months
With my wife and family. My eldest
Uncle, John, left me an estate
In land near Epping. I set my cattle
Down and left them to graze
      On a bowling green in Greenwich.

HEAD

Now he's worried that she'll wake
And discover this secret
That he's kept – that sometimes
In the night he lifts
Her head to feel its weight.

And even if the weight feels right
(A water-melon) he'll shake
It gently from side to side
And listen for the rattle
Of anything within, check,

Even if it's silent,
That it's securely shut,
That there's not some catch
Or hinged bit that's left
Undone for anything to get out.

And even if it's manifestly closed
He'll tap it once or twice
With knuckles tentative and white
And listen for an answering noise
Coming back across the space.

And, having completed this routine,
He'll repeat it just once
To make sure he didn't
Dream the soundlessness,
That he has a waking sense

That she is filled. But then
The moment always drags
When he sets down her head,
Like a waiter brimful with drinks,
Or as if he was handling eggs.

DR PROFUNDO

I shouldn't have looked into his eyes
But somehow they just drew me in.
That's how I was hypnotised.

His services were advertised-
Does your memory sometimes let you down?
I shouldn't have looked into his eyes.

I'd thought it was a pack of lies,
I'd thought he was a charlatan.
That's how I was hypnotised.

And the memories came like butterflies
Across the meadows of my brain,
I shouldn't have looked into his eyes,

And seen my life so summarised,
Every error and every sin,
That's how I was hypnotised.

And now I want it all revised,
It's hell recalling everything
I shouldn't have looked into his eyes,
That how I was hypnotised.

ECOPOESIS

Now it is time that gods emerge
from things by which we dwell ...

Rilke

1. Mirrors

The sky had nested itself in the rocks,
The regolith, the frozen poles.
They had digested its curled-up weather,
Its soufflé sunsets and Pavlova hurricanes
Locked in sub-surface cupboards of ice
Well beyond the nip of our tools.

Being vain men ourselves, our first
Thoughts were of mirrors, fleets
Of them hanging in the sky
To redirect and concentrate the sunshine,
And when they were built – a vast
Necklace of reflecting pearls in orbit,
Made from the scraps of sails,
Shafts of holy light appeared,
The sort that might bring simple
Shepherds to their knees
But which failed to convert
A single pebble of that
Endless beach. After fifty years
We took the mirrors
Out of their echelons
And sewed them together to make
Just two huge patchwork quilts
Of silver, each the size of the state
Of Michigan, focusing all
Their vicarious light on the poles.

At certain times, if the incline
Was right, a telescope would reveal
A planet multiplied by double reflection –
Trailing off like beads on a string into the curved
Darkness of space. A good sign, we thought,
The first step to an infinite universe
Of habitable worlds.

When the mirrors failed to fill
With more than a puddle
The depressions of the minor deserts,
Our third plan was put into action.
We found the hypothesised asteroids
Out beyond the orbit of Saturn
Wandering lamely like demented
Children in trouble with their guardians
And dressed in torn frocks of ice,
Rich in ammonia, which gave them
A lemony blush, as though a crop
Of daffodils had appeared in this
Little quarter of the infinite.
We strapped our nuclear rockets
To their backsides and let them
Fart across the parsecs until
They crashed on Mars – thump
Thump. They sprinkled the arid
Plains with their valuable, volatile
Salts and compounds, disturbing
The sleep of the sky as it lay still.
The proto-colonies had long since left
And we witnessed a landscape shift,
Dusty weather clearing to reveal
The impacted prospects,
The new lowlands where ranges
Had been, and a shock of orange
Liquid brimming in the remembered
Courses. The rivers went where rivers
Had been, redefining the estuaries
And islands with sharp, golden shores.
We'd refilled the drained cup
Of the oceans, a trillion tons of water
Converged on a bed the size of Connecticut,
And we cast our nets in a sea of piss.
So much, we thought, for ecopoesis.

3. The Factories

Having done our violence,
Within sight of the tear-drop shaped
River Islands south of the Elysium
Volcanoes, out beyond the sulphur
Scablands and the potassium forests
We built our first factories.
They sat like any factories
Though fashioned out of native materials,
With silica and quartz-encrusted
Fumaroles they looked like colossal,
Empty evening gowns
Standing alone in the desert,
And had no product,
Only by-product, the halocarbons
We longed for, the CFCs,
The cocktails of halogens,
Fluorine, chlorine, bromine, iodine,
The redeeming pollution. It took
So much work to produce
The necessary filth, our complex grew
To the size of Maryland, trainloads
Of matter every day, trainloads
Of refined waste leaving, a workcrew
Of thousands, as if bred for the sole
Purpose, and yet looking at those
Sequined chimneys you couldn't swear
That anything was happening
Until one day we noticed how the air
Began to weigh heavily on us,
How we each began to feel that we
Were carrying a small child on our shoulders,
A little, grey-haired girl called
Barometric Pressure who told us
We had at last fastened the atmosphere
To the planet and that we could go
Naked for the first time in centuries.

4. New Forms of Architecture

From poor Mars to rich Mars,
But the only enduring thing we had
Was our language. We pitched tents
Of it. We shepherded information,
Penned and stalled ideas, farmed
Conversation, planted orchards
Of discussion which fruited,
Ripened then fell, spawning
New lines of thought, of argument.
And sometimes our talk
Was a shed of crumpled tin
And sometimes a limestone
Cathedral, until by the time
We had the chance to build
Something permanent, we felt
Almost afraid for the demolition
Of our own history, word by word.
And this made us shy from the question –
How should our cities look?

Until then our habitats had been
Mere attachments, things pegged,
Clipped, riveted or bolted
To the surface, memos on a planetary
Noticeboard, but when we had
The chance to work with stone,
To embed ourselves with foundations
And cellarage, we found ourselves
Reverting to classical forms, the old
Orders – columns, pediments,
Entablatures, scrolled finials,
Pilasters, though we lacked
The essential tools and skills
To make our parthenons anything
But rough-hewn, wonky
Approximations of venerable

Geometries – like Cornish mansions
Our schemes had all the ambition
But none of the craft.
Some of us planned to build
Venice from an old book,
As an island city it seemed
Strangely appropriate, palaces
Teetering on a brink, but it was enough
To have the idea only, its execution
Seemed neither necessary nor possible.

And we sided in the end with those
Who wanted to shake the habit
Of being human and take the chance
To start afresh and let our buildings
Somehow grow like the green corn
That had taken so well, that we should
Farm our houses and let their form
Be determined by their time and place.
And so the ancient cities of Earth
Made their reappearance.
We still had our bodies, that
Was the problem. Houses are somatic,
Born from our dimensions and habits,
Ur, Nineveh, Babylon, their dumpy
Ziggurats, trailing plantlife, floods . . .
It took our cities to remind us
We were human.

5. We Were Pedestrians

We called them the Icarus Years
Because nearly every day
A boy would fall out of the sky,
And girls, their parents,
Uncles, Grand Uncles, whole
Families, sometimes several
In one day, sometimes the sky
Was a weeping mosaic of silver
Parachutes falling slowly,
Seriously, the airbags bouncing
Unpredictably in market squares,
Scattering geese and goats, landing
Sometimes in a fountain or fish pond,
To then hatch with a sound of zips
And Velcro unfastening (how touching
Those sounds), and out they'd step,
Carrying a sack of photos and keepsakes,
A chair, the odd statue, and always
A packet of seeds.

It took the average factory worker
A thousand years to earn enough money
To emigrate to Mars, so that it was
Only the rich who fell from the sky.
Money travels just one way through space.
Perhaps that accounted for the looks
Of horror on their faces when they
Discovered how we lived, as goatherds,
Burlap-wearing scratchers of livings,
Bearded, Biblical, folksy. They were shocked
To find we were pedestrians. Mars
Was to have been a gateway to an infinite
Universe of habitable worlds, they
Told us, and look what you've done.
Where there could have been space ports,
Universities, bridgeheads to miracles

Exploiting low gravity and untold
Mineral wealth, there were chickens,
Cathedrals on crutches, mucky
Compounds. They lectured us
On economics, reminded us
That the ecopoesis of Mars consumed more
Of Earth's energy than was used
From the founding of the Roman
Republic to the birth of The Beatles.
Of course, that was before
They'd seen the maize we'd cultivated
In green swathes all across
The Basin of Hellas, or the vineyards
That thrived on the tongue-shaped
Lava flows of the Tharsis volcanoes,
Or the lupin fields that dressed
With pink and purple skirts
The giant Olympus Mons.
They remembered the old pictures,
The bouldery tracts, courtyards
Of nothing, Empires of Emptiness.
They knew they would never
Want to go back.

6. Flora, Fauna, Geography

It was good to have new geography,
New shapes on the maps
To have so much to name
On the small, local scale of things.
We soon knew our way round.
The yellow lake (called *Yellow Lake*)
With its crystallised shores, almost
Named itself, as did the hill
In the shape of Brian's nose
(Called *Brian's Nose*). All this was new
And varied, and meaningful,
But when it came to animal
And plant life, we have to admit
We lack variety. So far, our ways
Are birdless. Try carrying an egg
From Earth to Mars without
Breaking it and you'll see how
Difficult it is. And fledged birds
Cannot cope with zero gravity,
I've heard how they beat
Their wings to no effect, to fall
And drift regardless was something
Neither hawks nor nightingales
Could cope with. Insects were easier,
They came in boxes freeze dried,
Like gravel, though one had to remember
To pack a packet of the seeds of their
Feeding matter. So we planted nettle groves
For the butterflies, dock, rock rose, gorse,
But it is an edited evolution we enjoy,
The minimum needed to sustain
An eco system, we make up for
The absence by a burgeoning of fairytales.
And we tell our own histories
Over and over. My father, and my
Grandfather, dealt in horses — shoed them,

Broke them, sold them at fairs
In the fields beneath Neil Armstrong.
My mother sold milk and butter.
Her people were pig breeders
In Nixon where the pink rills bubble
And the downfall glitters on the plateau.

7. Looking Back

The last millionaires fell from the sky
A century ago. They brought with them
Sad stories of the lives they had left,
How a belief in unicorns and mermaids
Had revived, how the cities had been
Consumed by privet and laurel,
Of sickness, reforestation, wars of religion.

Our children listened entranced
And filled with longing to be
In the world of islands with all
Its rich, rewarding dangers.

Our atmosphere factories have begun
To take on something of the mystery
And charm of pyramids, though
They remind me more of coffee pots,
Or cafetières, and the pillowy mountains
Behind them with the croissant-shaped
Pebbles that strew their slopes always
Remind me that what we have made here
Is one vast room, world-sized,
Near whose ceiling two acorn
Moons float. Sofa hills. Lamp-stand mountain.
You have to keep a sense of proportion.

Last week the mirrors were ripped
To shreds as they re-entered the atmosphere,
And poured their mirrory rain over a field
The size of the state of Missouri.

THE ROLLER

It was one of those things
Left by the previous owner,
His rusty hand-me-down that must
Have once levelled the lawns
That we let grow.

One enormous wheel set between
The branching forks of a shaft,
Fused to a single lump of iron fixed
At the far, rarely visited end of the garden,
As though it had just fallen out of the sky,
Something lent by the gods to hammer
Our garden into shape, or, with its
Vertical stem, a germinating tulip bulb
Fallen from their nursery.

A few times it took on the duties of a rocking horse,
Hardly noticing our childish weight
As we pushed the handle back and forth
To set a tipsy motion going, enough
To lever up the frozen hub and reveal
A concave underworld of pressed earth
Inset with worms. I think of it now
As something falling too slowly for the eye to see,
Deeper and deeper into the garden. At other times
I could flip it like a shuttlecock over
The feeble blossom of the toffee-apple tree.

Its last moments were a half broomstick
Pushed through the slot where the old handle
Had rotted away, and the whole thing pulled
By three of us the length of the garden
To the skip that waited. Proud of our adult strength
We'd opened up old wounds. A flattened stripe
Of disturbance like a scorch mark cancelling
The garden from end to end.